Executive Summary

Sexual Risk Avoidance (SRA), an abstinence-centered approach to sex education, is the best public health strategy to prevent unintended teen pregnancies and sexually-transmitted infections (STIs). Designed to emphasize risk *avoidance*, rather than risk *reduction*, SRA programs are based on effective programs designed to encourage teens to avoid underage drinking, illicit drug use, reckless driving, and other risky behaviors. It sends a clear message that abstinence is the healthiest choice that teens can make for themselves and for society as a whole, and it presents that message in a dignified, age-appropriate manner.

Comprehensive Sex Education (CSE) is an alternative approach designed to teach all options related to sexual behavior. The model is based on the presumption that sexual behavior after puberty is inevitable. Preteens and teens learn a range of information related to anatomy, human reproduction, the use of contraceptives, and the risks of pregnancy and STIs associated with having sex. They also learn about relationships and the personal skills needed to reduce risk.[1]

By contrast, SRA is guided by the most current adolescent behavioral theory and optimal health. It emphasizes risk avoidance as the best choice to prevent an unplanned pregnancy. Although SRA provides information on contraception, the central message is that abstinence is the best choice for teens. Lessons and activities are age-appropriate and designed to help teens make and keep a commitment to being abstinent. The support of parents and other guardians is important to these programs.[2]

CSE continues to be the most widely available sex education model in the United States due in large part to Federal funding. Similar to the earlier medical model of sex education, CSE takes a value-neutral approach to teenage sexual behavior. Although it provides information on the benefits of abstinence, it also teaches ways to prevent an unplanned pregnancy. It is, therefore, non-directive in helping teens to make the most age-appropriate and healthy choice. The underlying message of CSE to both parents and teens is that abstinence may be an effective choice, but that teens cannot or will not abstain from sex. As a result, the core message is risk reduction.[3]

The prevalence of CSE has led many parents and taxpayers to perceive it as the best approach. Decades of evaluation tell another story. CSE has done little in the last 20 years to impact rates of teenage pregnancy.[4] An updated approach, SRA, is demonstrating effectiveness by emulating theory-based and successful public health campaigns helping teens set and keep

---

[1]National Guideline Task Force. *Guidelines for Comprehensive Sexuality Education K-12- 3rd Edition.* Sexuality Information and Education Council of the United States (SIECUS). 2004. http://www2.gsu.edu/~wwwche/Sex%20ed%20class/guidelines.pdf.

[2] Ikramullah, E., Manlove, J., Cui, C. and Moore, K. Parents Matter: *The role of Parents in Teens' Decisions about Sex.* Washington, DC: Child Trends, Child Trends. 2009 http://www.childtrends.org/Files/Child_Trends-2009_11_11_RB_Parents&TeenSex.pdf.

[3] http://www.thecommunityguide.org/hiv/supportingmaterials/ISriskreduction.html.

[4] Moore, K.A. and Sugland, B.W. (2001) Next Steps and Best Bets: Approaches to Preventing Adolescent Childbearing. Washington, DC: Child Trends.(http://www.childtrends.org/files/Child_Trends-1996_01_01_ES_NextSteps.pdf).

short-and long-term goals, and involving parents. Critically important to effectiveness, SRA is also age appropriate.[5]

This report demonstrates that SRA is the better approach because it comports with the latest research on teenage behavior and fosters healthy development. CSE has failed to lower rates of teenage pregnancy because it assumes that preteens and teens are fully capable of making decisions without adequate guidance. By contrast, a clear understanding of teenage behavior is why public health campaigns against teenage drinking, smoking, and reckless driving have been relatively successful. They are not value neutral when it comes to teenage choices, especially those with public health ramifications. These programs set realistic and age-appropriate expectations for the teens and then show them how to avoid the risky behaviors. SRA is modeled on that successful reasoning. Research suggests that building the Federal effort to prevent teenage pregnancy on the SRA model would lead to a greater success than the CSE model has been able to achieve over the past two decades.

This report also clarifies the role of evaluation in prevention programs. Outcome evaluation is an important tool. However, that stage of research is not enough to determine the success of a program. Evaluation, simply put, is a comparison between a strategic plan and the actual impacts of that plan. Programs must first be planned and designed around sound theory and current findings that are explicitly stated. Without that guidance, it is difficult to design an effective program or to effectively evaluate its results. Then programs must be implemented consistent with the plan. Outcome evaluation then measures the program impact. Evaluation conducted throughout the process of program development improves quality and effectiveness, so that findings will be able to adequately inform policy making.

---

[5] *Jemmott, J. B., Jemmott L. S.,Fong G. T. (2010).* Efficacy of a theory-based abstinence-only intervention over 24 months. *Arch Pediatr Adolesc Med. 2010;164(2):152-159.*

I. <u>Background</u>

Federal Involvement in Sex Education

Federal funding for sex education programs began in the 1960s and 1970s. Legislative initiatives, including Titles V, XIX, and XX of the Social Security Act and Title X of the Public Health Service Act, were created in part to address poverty caused by unplanned pregnancy and fears of overpopulation. Federal funding made it possible for the poor to access primary healthcare and family planning services. Primary prevention programs were designed to teach about the biological aspects of sexuality and contraception. Taking a value-neutral and non-directive approach to the morality of premarital sex, these programs became a permanent fixture in the fight against teenage pregnancy. Today, these programs have evolved into a hybrid called comprehensive sex education (CSE) that includes building self-esteem, decision making skills, and other social factors. Like the early programs, CSE continues to teach that contraception is the best protection against an unplanned pregnancy.[6]

By 1980, as the number of sexually active teens grew, rates of teen pregnancy and sexually transmitted infections (STIs) began to rise. Many Americans believed that "value-neutral" sex education was responsible for the increase, and that teens needed guidance, and not just a "how-to" class to make healthy choices about their sexuality.[7] In response, Congress enacted the Adolescent Family Life Act (AFLA) to find ways of reaching adolescents before they become sexually active and to promote self-discipline and other prudent approaches to the problem of adolescent premarital sexual activity. AFLA further indicated that since the problems of adolescent premarital sexual activity, pregnancy, and parenthood are multiple and complex, such problems are best approached through a variety of integrated and essential services provided to adolescents and their families – instead of a strictly medical approach.[8]

AFLA angered proponents of the existing sex education approach. They believed that abstinence until marriage was an old-fashioned "chastity" program[9] "designed to control young people's sexual behavior by instilling fear and shame".[10] Opponents of AFLA suggested the approach was nothing more than religion masquerading as public health policy. They sued in *Bowen v. Kendrick*, alleging that AFLA was an unconstitutional establishment of religion, eventually losing that argument in the Supreme Court.[11] Even as rates of teenage pregnancy rose and more teens contracted STIs including HIV, AFLA opponents believed that teens would be

---

[6] Lord, Alexandra. (2009) <u>Condom Nation: The U.S. Government's Sex Education Campaign from World War I to the Internet</u>. The Johns Hopkins University Press.

[7] Lickona, Thomas. "Where Sex Education Went Wrong. Character Education November 1993 Vol 51 Number 3 pages 84-89. And Moran, Jeffrey. (2002). <u>Teaching Sex: The Shaping of Adolescence in the 20th Century</u>. Cambridge and London:Harvard University Press.

[8] "Reauthorization of the Adolescent Family Life Demonstration Projects Act of 1981". Hearings before the Subcommittee on Family and Human Services of the Committee on Labor and Human Resources United States Senate. April 24, 1984.

[9] http://www.plannedparenthood.org/about-us/who-we-are/history-and-successes.htm.

[10] http://www.futureofsexed.org/background.html.

[11] Donovan, P. "The Adolescent Family Life Act and the Promotion of Religious Doctrine". Fam Plann Perspective, 1984 Sept-Oct; 16(5) 222-8.

protected as long as they had information about their sexuality and access to contraception.[12] The battle over control of sex education continues today as part of a larger more deeply entrenched culture war over the politics of sex with abstinence as one of its targets.[13]

The Impact of Abstinence Education

AFLA survived and, with the emergence of HIV-AIDS, the abstinence message gained greater acceptance. By the 1990s, some public health groups believed that it was a good strategy to counter the spread of HIV-AIDS.[14] It was also embraced by many parents and teens who feared the consequences of premarital sexual activity and STIs. As a result, after 20 years of steady increases, the rate of teenage pregnancy began to decline and continued to decline for the next decade.[15] In 1996, Congress provided funding to expand abstinence programs with the enactment of the Title V abstinence education program in the 1996 Welfare Reform Act.[16]

Faced with the fact that abstinence was both popular and effective,[17] proponents of the existing model of sex education modified their strategy. The new approach was a hybrid of the two competing messages: be abstinent and, if you do not choose abstinence, use medical protection to reduce your risk of pregnancy and disease. Programs were expanded to include lessons on decision making and social activities to reinforce the message. The new design was called comprehensive sex education (CSE) and was heralded as the new answer to teenage pregnancy by its designers. To supporters of abstinence, it was a dangerous mixed message.

The Obama Administration Shifts Federal Funding to CSE

The Teenage Pregnancy Prevention (TPP) initiative, the Pregnancy Assistance Fund, and the Personal Responsibility Education Program (PREP) are three initiatives promoted by the Obama Administration to combat teenage pregnancy. With over $200 million available, the Department of Health and Human Services (HHS) selected 31 CSE programs (and one SRA program) that it describes as models of prevention with "proven" results. It is using these existing programs as the basis for funding new programs. HHS hopes to address "rising teen

---

[12] Donovan, P. "School-Based Sexuality Education: The Issues and Challenges". Family Planning Perspectives, 1998 July/August; 30(4):188-93.

[13] Irvine, J. (2002). Talk About Sex: The battles over Sex Education in the United States . Berkeley and Los Angeles:University of California Press.

[14] Jemmott, JB, Jemmott, LS, Fong, GT (1998). "Abstinence and safer sex HIV risk-reduction for African American adolescents: a randomized controlled study trial". JAMA 1998 May 20;279 (19):1529-36.

[15] Mohn JK, Tingle LR and Finger R, "An analysis of the causes of the decline in non-marital birth and pregnancy rates for teens from 1991 to 1995," *Adolescent and Family Health,* 2002, 3(1):39-47.
 Darroch JE and Singh S, *Why is Teenage Pregnancy Declining? The Roles of Abstinence, Sexual Activity and Contraceptive Use,* Occasional Report, New York: The Alan Guttmacher Institute, 1999,No. 1.

[16] http://www.welfareacademy.org/conf/past/haskins2.shtml.
Staff report of the United States House of Representatives Committee on Government Reform. "Abstinence and its Critics". October, 2006.

[17] Abma, J.C., Chandra, A., Mosher, W., Peterson, L., & Piccinino, L. (1997). "Fertility, Family Planning, and Women's Health: New Data from the 1995 National Survey of Family Growth." National Center for Health Statistics Vital Health Statistics 23(19).

pregnancy rates by supporting grantees in replicating evidence-based models" and making sure that programs are medically accurate and age-appropriate.[18]

The *Aban Aya Youth Program* was selected by HHS as an evidence-based and age-appropriate CSE program worthy of replication. The program is an Afrocentric social development approach that uses a curriculum administered over a four year period to children in grades 5-8. Students receive 16-21 lessons per year that include information on sexual behavior and related topics, such as violence and substance abuse. The curriculum encourages both abstinence and safe sex. Teachers received no formal training for implementing the program. When the program ended at completion of the eighth grade, data collected from student surveys showed that boys were significantly less likely than the boys in the control group to report recent sexual intercourse. The study found no impact on sexual intercourse for girls.[19]

This program is not ready to be replicated for many reasons. First, the study was undermined when students were added after random assignment. Second, the program was not effective with girls. And even though the results for the boys were significant, that finding was based on self-reporting, a method that can be unreliable with children and teens.

The biggest problem with the program is its design, which falls beyond the scope of the evaluation. The median age of the children in this study was 10.8 years. Yet, they were asked to openly discuss and report sexual intercourse. Few researchers, child development experts, and most parents would describe this method as age-appropriate. On the contrary, they would caution against using this approach with children who have not reached puberty.

The *Aban Aya Youth Program* has many of the same problems as the other evidence-based models recommended by HHS. Results were dependent on self-reporting measurements. Teens did not use risk reduction methods, such as contraception, consistently. Positive outcomes were not sustained for more than six months or a year. Preteens were exposed to mature material, such as safe sex methods, and asked to discuss and report sexual behavior and contraceptive use. Nevertheless, the Obama Administration praised the program and thought it deserved replication.

Despite strong evidence that abstinence is the healthiest and most effective choice, proponents of CSE continue to argue that abstinence education programs are not effective. They believe that teens should not have sex, but cannot be discouraged from having it. Therefore, they simply need medically accurate information and access to contraception to protect them.[20] Thus equipped, CSE proponents believe that teens will make sound choices about their sexual behavior. Yet, despite decades of research and a massive infusion of Federal funds into this strategy, there is little evidence to support that claim.

---

[18] http://www.hhs.gov/ash/oah/oah-initiatives/tpp.
[19] http://www.hhs.gov/ash/oah/oah-initiatives/tpp/programs/aban_aya_youth_project.pdf.
[20] http://www.guttmacher.org/pubs/FB-ATSRH.html.

II. A Better Approach to Prevention

Often overlooked in the debate over teenage pregnancy prevention, and certainly overwhelmed by the practical burdens of what is a serious public health issue, is an American teenager. Although the social policy and economic ramifications of 750,000 pregnant teens per year are substantial, each of these pregnancies is about an actual teen and his or her ability to manage the complicated risks associated with premarital sexual behavior and how to shoulder the real possibility of an unwanted pregnancy. The decisions and factors that influence these issues are components of the larger problem – a point first recognized in AFLA. And if solutions are to be found, they must focus on the factors that produce sexual activity and pregnancy among teens. In short, the solution is to find the best approach to protecting teens from high risk behavior.

Researchers and experts in adolescent behavior have been studying teenage risk taking for decades. Since risk is a key factor in teenage pregnancy prevention and a key difference between the SRA approach and CSE approach, theory and research can help determine the better approach. SRA takes a risk avoidance approach to teenage sexual behavior and presents abstinence as the best choice. CSE maintains that teen sexual behavior is inevitable and that teens need to learn risk reduction to avoid unwanted pregnancies. To identify the better approach, three questions need to be addressed:

1. What do the experts tells us about adolescents and risk taking?
2. What protects teens as they learn to negotiate risk?
3. How do successful public health prevention programs deal with teenage risk?

What Do the Experts Tell Us About Adolescents and Risk Taking?

Young people experience profound physical, cognitive, and emotional changes during adolescence. The physical changes are the most obvious, but other changes during adolescence are equally significant, especially those that challenge personal identity and emotional independence. Teenage thinking can be egocentric and unrealistic with little appreciation for how things actually work. Teens test limits and take risks – behavior that is normal and useful during adolescence. However, for many, unsupervised and reckless behavior can often become too risky and even dangerous.[21]

In general, teens take more risks than younger and older individuals even as they lack the proper controls to manage them.[22] Behaviors, such as smoking, drinking, driving, and sexual activity involve considerable risk, especially for teens who have not mastered two important skills – planning and risk assessment.[23] According to Dr. Laurence Steinberg, Professor of Psychology at Temple University, the ability to regulate impulse, think ahead, plan, and weigh risk and reward develop gradually in a teen and are often not complete until the mid-twenties.[24]

---

[21] Steinberg, L. 2007. *Adolescence* (8th Edition). New York: McGraw-Hill.
[22] Steinberg, L. (2007) "Risk Taking in Adolescence: New perspectives from brain and behavioral science". *Current Directions in Psychological Science, 16, 2: pp. 55-59.*
[23] Steinberg, L. 2007. *Adolescence* (8th Edition). New York: McGraw-Hill.
[24] Steinberg, Laurence, Ph.D., The Basic Principles of Good Parenting. Simon & Schuster: New York, 2004.

High rates of underage drinking, car accidents, unplanned pregnancy and STIs among teens support the view that most teens are unable to manage the risks associated with these behavioral choices even when provided with warnings.[25]

Brain imaging provides new insights into how the teenage brain works. Using magnetic resonance imaging (MRI), neuroscientists have identified two networks in the frontal lobe of the brain that impact teenage behavior and choices. The social and emotional network is immediately changed with the onset of puberty and becomes very sensitive. The cognitive network that governs planning, thinking ahead, and self-regulation matures gradually. Under normal conditions, the cognitive network can regulate the social/emotional network. However, when the social/emotional network is highly activated, they do not work together. The emotional network dominates the cognitive network. The result is that emotion, rather than reason, often influences teen decision making.[26]

Adolescent development is not entirely determined by brain maturation. Teens are affected by social concerns: education, sports, work, friends, social networks, and other cultural influences. However, as they negotiate these concerns, often independent of their parents, they are frequently drawn to risk – like sexual behavior. Expecting preteens and teens to assess and reduce those risks by drawing on the medical information learned in a few sessions of CSE is inconsistent with both behavioral and neuroscientific research.[27]

What Protects Teens as They Learn to Negotiate Risk?

Teens navigate the challenges of adolescence primarily with the help of parents. As no one else can, parents attempt to make sure that their children stay centered and protected. Parental involvement is associated with educational success, improved health, positive self-esteem, and healthy relationships. Across the board, children who have a close relationship with their parents are less likely to have behavioral problems or engage in high risk behaviors.[28]

Parental involvement is also important in delaying sexual activity among teens. In a nationally representative poll of teens aged 12-19, nearly half (46 percent) reported that parents had the most influence on their decisions about sex.[29] In a study published by Child Trends, a group of researchers analyzed data from the National Longitudinal Survey of Youth and found that parental involvement is associated with delayed sex among teens. In general, parental

[25] De Guzman, MR. and Bosch, R. "High-Risk Behaviors Among Youth". NebGuide: University of Nebraska-Lincoln. 2007 http://www.ianrpubs.unl.edu/pages/publicationD.jsp?publicationId=786.

[26] Steinberg, L. (2007) "Risk Taking in Adolescence: New perspectives from brain and behavioral science". *Current Directions in Psychological Science, 16, 2: pp. 55-59.*

[27] http://www.sciencedaily.com/releases/2007/04/070412115231.htm.

[28] Miller B, Benson B, & Galbraith K, Family relationships and adolescent pregnancy risk: A research synthesis, *DevelopmentalReview,* 2001, 21(1): 1-38. And Borkowski JG, Ramey SL, & Bristol-Power M, *Parenting and the child's world: Influences on academic, intellectual,and social-emotional development.* Mahwah, NJ: Psychology Press, 2001. And

Kirby D, Lepore G, & Ryan J. *Sexual risk and protective factors: Factors affecting teen sexual behavior, pregnancy, childbearing, and sexually transmitted disease.* Washington,DC: National Campaign to Prevent Teen Pregnancy.

[29] The National Campaign to Prevent Teen Pregnancy. (2010) *With one voice2010: America's adults and teens sound off about teen pregnancy.* Washington, DC: Author.

involvement, including communication and monitoring, is associated with reduced risk of teenage pregnancy. [30]

Parents help their teens manage risk and reach their goals by monitoring and strengthening their sense of self-efficacy. Self-efficacy is the perception of one's ability to accomplish tasks and overcome the challenges presented in daily life. It plays a significant role in the growth of a teenager's self-esteem and resiliency, because it gives the teen a sense of autonomy and responsibility to handle stressful situations, to overcome disappointment, to ask for needed help, and to avoid risky behavior. [31]

It is therefore important for parents and others to monitor their teen's capability for handling responsibility. Parents help them to develop positive self-efficacy by giving them appropriate responsibilities. As capacity increases, so should responsibility. Successfully managing responsibility gives the teen a sense of competence. When teens cannot manage responsibility, failure can have the opposite effect -- delayed development. [32]

As developmental psychologists, educators, public health experts, and now neuroscientists have discovered, while teens are maturing physically and emotionally and becoming more independent, they are not yet adults. Teens need guidance to make healthy choices. As those choices get more risky and dangerous, guidance and limits from parents that are reinforced by peers, teachers, and other authority figures are critically important. [33]

How Do Successful Public Health Prevention Programs Deal with Teenage Risk?

Public health programs designed to encourage teens to avoid risk behaviors, such as underage drinking, illicit drug use, and reckless driving have several common elements:

- They work to achieve a maximum level of safety for the teen and the community.
- They encourage risk avoidance and ban or restrict participation in the risky behavior.
- Because of the inherent complexity of behavioral change, they include social-psychological activities that reinforce the healthy message.
- They encourage guidance, especially parental guidance that helps protect the teen.
- They are theory based and age appropriate.
- They rely on age-appropriate program design and rigorous evaluation to continuously monitor the success of the program -- if something does not work, new and more effective strategies are adopted.

---

[30] Ikramullah, E., Manlove, J. PhD, Cui, C. and Moore, K. *Parents Matter: The Role of Parents in Teens' Decisions about Sex*. Washington DC: Child Trends, 2009.

[31] Schunk, D. H., & Meece, J. (2005). Self-efficacy development in adolescence. In F. Pajares & T. Urdan (Eds.), *Self-efficacy beliefs during adolescence*. Greenwich, CT: Information Age Publishing. Acceptance Date: 2005 http://www.des.emory.edu/mfp/03SchunkMeeceAdoEd5.pdf.

[32] Schunk, D. H., & Meece, J. (2005). Self-efficacy development in adolescence. In F. Pajares & T. Urdan (Eds.), *Self-efficacy beliefs during adolescence*. Greenwich, CT: Information Age Publishing. Acceptance Date: 2005 http://www.des.emory.edu/mfp/03SchunkMeeceAdoEd5.pdf.

[33] De Guzman, MR. and Bosch, R. "High-Risk Behaviors Among Youth". NebGuide: University of Nebraska-Lincoln. 2007. http://www.ianrpubs.unl.edu/pages/publicationD.jsp?publicationId=786.

Among the public health prevention programs that have incorporated these elements are:

Preventing car accidents by teens –

- According to the CDC, the risk of motor vehicle crashes is higher among 16- to 19-year-olds than among any other age group. In fact, per mile driven, teen drivers ages 16 to 19 are four times more likely than older drivers to crash.[34]
- Strategies that were the most effective in reducing teenage car accidents are consistent with optimum health and the needs of teens. When lowering the age of driving below 16 years resulted in an increase in car accidents, States moved to increase the driving age and limited the number of passengers.[35]
- The most significant factor that affected teenage car accidents was parental involvement and guidance. Parents were encouraged to drive with their teens and to monitor the use of the car.[36]
- States are now moving to institute graduated driver licensing (GDL) systems that help new drivers gain skills under low-risk conditions. As drivers move through stages, they are given extra driving privileges.[37]

Preventing underage drinking –

- Underage drinking is a persistent public health issue that is related to other risk behaviors, such as tobacco use and car accidents.[38]
- In a study funded by the National Institute on Alcohol Abuse and Alcoholism, public health experts identified strategies to prevent underage drinking. Key factors included:[39]

  o Effective strategies should be based on behavioral theory and an understanding of risk and protective factors.
  o Parents should monitor children's activities during adolescence.
  o Extracurricular activities should be supervised by positive adult role models.
  o Building self-efficacy is an important protective factor.

Preventing teen tobacco use –

- Efforts to prevent teenage smoking have been successful as rates have dropped steadily since 1999.[40]

---

[34]http://www.cdc.gov/Motorvehiclesafety/Teen_Drivers/ and Insurance Institute for Highway Safety (IIHS). Fatality facts: teenagers 2008. Arlington (VA): The Institute; 2009 [cited 2009 Nov 3].

[35] http://usnews.rankingsandreviews.com/cars-trucks/daily-news/080909-Safety-Group-Wants-to-Raise-Driving-Age.

[36]http://www.cdc.gov/ParentsAreTheKey/pdf/factsheets/ParentsGetTheFacts-a.pdf..

[37] http://www.cdc.gov/ParentsAreTheKey/licensing/index.html.

[38] http://www.cdc.gov/alcohol/fact-sheets/underage-drinking.htm.

[39] Komro, KA., Toomey, T. "Strategies to Prevent Underage Drinking". Alcohol Res Health. 202;26(1):5-14 http://pubs.niaaa.nih.gov/publications/arh26-1/5-14.htm.

[40]Youth Risk Behavior Survey; Surgeon General's report in http://www.washingtonpost.com/national/health-science/tobacco-use-among-teenagers/2012/03/07/gIQAdQrByR_graphic.html.

- Despite some periodic fluctuations, U.S. consumption of cigarettes has declined by more than 100 billion cigarettes in the last decade, and per capita consumption has declined steadily since 1963.[41]
- To achieve these results, different strategies were tried and tested over many years, but the main goal of the campaigns was simple – avoid the risk and quit smoking.[42]
- The CDC's Community Preventive Services Task Force analyzed the different strategies used in tobacco control and listed the most effective strategies in reducing smoking.[43]

  o Their recommendations include both risk avoidance and regular guidance.
  o They support programs that are comprehensive and multi-faceted and include social activities to reinforce prevention.
  o In addition, they promote the use of individual guidance and regular reminders, such as telephone quit-lines.
  o And, they recommend strategies designed to avoid risk, such as banning the sale of tobacco products to teens.

<u>Risk messaging in the context of emergency preparedness</u> –

Risk messaging is an important factor in emergency preparedness, because citizens must understand and act on disaster warnings. Fitzpatrick and Miletti, in their work on risk communication, stress that people do need information in a high risk situation. However, that information will not necessarily change behavior, unless five critical steps take place. People must:

1. Hear the information
2. Understand the information
3. Believe the information
4. Personalize the information
5. Act on the information

Getting from step 1 to step 5 is more than a simple educational process. It is a highly interactive process. Information must be explained, verified and reinforced by others, when it is needed most – at the time of risk. Guidance must be available to ensure that a warning is not only heard, but that it is also personalized and acted upon. That messaging is critical to protecting the public from risk and harm.[44]

These public health campaigns to encourage teens to avoid risk behaviors share common factors that are supported by behavioral theory and rigorous evaluation. The programs are value-based as teens were encouraged to make the healthiest choice by avoiding the risky behavior. At

---

[41]Report of the American Lung Association. "Trends in Tobacco Use". July, 2011. http://www.lung.org/finding-cures/our-research/trend-reports/Tobacco-Trend-Report.pdf.

[42]http://www.cdc.gov/tobacco/tobacco_control_programs/surveillance_evaluation/key_outcome/pdfs/Chapter2.pdfttp.

[43] Report of the community Preventive Services Task Force. "First Annual Report to Congress: The Community Guide". 2011 http://www.thecommunityguide.org/library/ARC2011/congress-report-full.pdf..

[44] Fitzpatrick C. Mileti DS. Public risk communication. In Dynes RR, Tierney, KJ. Editors. Disasters, collective behavior, and social organization. Newark (NJ): University of Delaware Press; 1994, p. 71-84.

the same time, efforts were made to help build the capacity of the teen using guidance and low risk activities. Activities were age-appropriate and dignified. Programs showed effectiveness in getting the teen to adopt the healthy behavior and in reducing national rates of smoking and reckless driving.

Lesson Learned – SRA Is the Better Approach

SRA is a better approach to prevent teenage pregnancy than CSE, because it is informed by the best available knowledge base. Even though CSE has some good components, SRA is more grounded in behavioral theory and research, and it incorporates the strategies that have been successful in other youth risk programs. With a clear message that abstinence is the best and safest choice for teens, SRA promotes optimal health. An abstinence choice ensures that teens will avoid risky sexual behavior that they are not prepared to handle. SRAs include protective factors, especially the involvement of parents and other guardians. The values present in SRA programs are consistent with views of parents and the community at large. SRA is age-appropriate and presents sensitive information in a dignified manner. SRA holds the promise of finally impacting the incidence of teenage pregnancy and STIs.

III. Evaluation

Background on Evaluation

Sex education programs in the 1970s had never demonstrated an impact on teenage behavior. It was a purely educational model that was effective in increasing knowledge, but inadequate in actually changing behavior.[45] In addition, these programs did not impact pregnancy trends and appeared to make the problem worse. From 1970-1990 as the number of these programs increased, so did the rates of teenage pregnancy.[46]

By the 1990s, evaluation of sex education became more rigorous. CSE programs showed some progress in changing teenage attitudes and behavior related to sex. However, these results were often limited and non-sustained. In its forward to the 2007 report, *Emerging Answers: Research Findings on Programs to Reduce Teen Pregnancy and Sexually Transmitted Diseases,* the National Campaign to Prevent Teen and Unplanned Pregnancy stated that "many of these (CSE) programs—even those deemed effective—often have only modest results, many are fragile and poorly-funded, and most of these programs serve only a fraction of all the kids in the area who are at risk."[47]

Evaluation of abstinence programs did not begin in earnest until 1996 when Congress authorized $50 million to evaluate their effectiveness. Once completed, these evaluations found

---

[45] Mayer-Mihalski, N.& DeLuca, MJ. "Effective Education Leading to Behavior Change".White Paper: ParagonRX. May,2009(http://www.paragonrx.com/experience/white-papers/effective-education-leading-to-behavior-change/).

[46] Boonstra, H. Teen "Pregnancy:Trends and Lessons Learned". The Guttmacher Report on Public Policy February 2002, Vol 5, No.1. "http://www.guttmacher.org/pubs/tgr/05/1/gr050107.html.

[47]Kirby D, *Emerging Answers 2007: Research Findings on Programs to Reduce Teen Pregnancy and Sexually Transmitted Diseases*, Washington, DC: The National Campaign to Prevent Teen and Unplanned Pregnancy, 2007 http://www.thenationalcampaign.org/EA2007/EA2007_sum.pdf.

that abstinence programs also did not demonstrate an effect on teenage sexual behavior. However, more recent abstinence programs, called Sexual Risk Avoidance (SRA) model are demonstrating effectiveness (see Appendix).

For both CSE and SRA, the evaluation models currently in place – typically relying only on an outcome evaluation – lack key elements of an effective evaluation strategy. In order to develop meaningful measurements of these programs' impact on teenage behavior and attitudes, a more comprehensive approach to evaluation is needed.

A Better Approach to Evaluation

Although outcome evaluation is very important, this one stage of an evaluation process depends on successful completion of other stages, such as the planning and development of a program. Evaluation is simply a comparison between a strategic plan and the actual impacts of that plan.[48] A program plan must be informed by theory that explicitly and accurately identifies the central question to be examined – the hypothesis. A good evaluation begins during the planning stage, continues through implementation, and concludes with an understanding of why a program succeeded or failed.[49]

The debate about the best approach to teenage pregnancy prevention has centered on one aspect of evaluation, the outcome evaluation, even though program planning and development also need to be evaluated. Planning begins with the identification of the assumptions, goals, objectives, and methods that are guided by theory and the best available research. For sex education, the theory base is adolescent development and the vehicle for achieving the goals and objectives is a curriculum. To ensure that the curriculum is well-designed, the content should be reviewed by experts in adolescent development, parents, teachers, and even teens by conducting a form of evaluation called field testing.

One of the biggest reasons that programs fail can be traced to the improper delivery of services. A process evaluation is a way to determine if and how the program was delivered. Monitoring determines if the services, such as sex education, are delivered according to the program plan. Or, as often happens when programs are offered at multiple locations by different teachers, a process evaluation can determine if the services were implemented consistently. For sex education programs, teachers are a key to proper implementation. It is important that they receive training on how to implement the curriculum to avoid variation that can impact findings.[50]

With proper planning and program delivery, the findings from an outcome evaluation, if correctly designed, will be more reliable. They can be used to understand the effect of the

[48] Rossi, PH., Freeman, HE., and Wright, SR. (1979). *Evaluation: A Systematic Approach*. Beverly Hills, CA:Sage Publications.
[49] Rossi, PH., Freeman, HE., and Wright, SR. (1979). *Evaluation: A Systematic Approach*. Beverly Hills, CA:Sage Publications.
[50] Rossi, PH., Freeman, HE., and Wright, SR. (1979). *Evaluation: A Systematic Approach*. Beverly Hills, CA:Sage Publications.

program. In addition, they provide the confidence needed to determine if a program can be improved or replicated.[51]

Central to the evaluation process are the explicit assumptions that are used to identify the hypothesis being tested. If the assumptions are not drawn from the best available theoretical and empirical information, it will be difficult to control the quality of the program and evaluate its effectiveness.[52] And, even if some objectives are met, without explicit assumptions, there is no understanding of why the program worked or did not work.

CSE programs have shown some modest success over the last 20 years, yet they never live up to the hope of consistently impacting rates of teenage pregnancy.[53] Why? Because they are guided by the wrong assumptions. For example, even though experts believe that teens lack certain executive functions, CSE assumes that teens armed with "accurate" medical information and interpersonal skills are able to assess the risk involved with sexual activity and disease prevention. In addition, CSE assumes that teens cannot or will not practice abstinence which is not consistent with the evidence that most teens are choosing abstinence.[54] There is a disconnect between theory and assumption or cause and effect in CSE programs that leads to choosing ineffective strategies. As a result, CSE programs, even with those that have shown a modest effect, do little to inform how and why the change occurred.[55]

Rigorous outcome evaluation is the "gold standard" for determining cause, but it works best when it is aligned with other evaluation steps. Planning and evaluation are needed to adequately inform program development. The planning process ensures that the goals, objectives, and methods for the program are grounded in theory and the best available research. Evaluation is used to determine the effectiveness of the program. In the case of sex education programs, outcome evaluation alone, even if it is rigorous, cannot produce the findings needed to inform policy making. Good evaluation begins with good planning and faithful implementation of a well-designed program.

IV. Conclusions and Recommendations

America's teens need guidance to protect them from the consequences of risky sexual behavior. Unfortunately, the current course of national policy on teenage pregnancy prevention is undermining the desired health outcome. Careful examination of research confirms that a value-neutral and risk reduction approach to sexual behavior is not consistent with teenage

---

[51]Rossi, PH., Freeman, HE., and Wright, SR. (1979). *Evaluation: A Systematic Approach.* Beverly Hills, CA:Sage Publications.

[52] Rossi, PH., Freeman, HE., and Wright, SR. (1979). *Evaluation: A Systematic Approach.* Beverly Hills, CA:Sage Publications.

[53] Oringanje C., Meremikwu MM, Eko H, Esu, E, Meremikwu a, Ehiri JE. "Interventions for preventing unintended pregnancies among adolescents". The Cochrane Collaboration, The Cochrane Library 2010, Issue 1: Wiley Publishers.

[54] Centers for Disease Control(2011). Trends in the prevalence of sexual behaviors:National YRBS:1991-2009. Atlanta:CDC. Assessed August 28,2011 at http://www.cdc.gov/healthyyouth/yrbs/pdf/us_sexual_trend_yrbs.pdf.

[55]Reeve, J; Peerbhoy, D. (2007). "Evaluating the evaluation: Understanding the utility and limitations of evaluation as a tool for organizational learning". *Health Education Journal* 66 (2): 120–131.

behavioral theory and not effective in impacting America's high rates of teenage pregnancy and STIs.

A better approach is needed that incorporates the capability of teens to manage risk in the same way as programs designed to prevent teenage smoking, underage drinking, and reckless driving. Teens are confused by messages that are non-directive about risking taking and optimal health. Instead, they need programs that encourage healthy choices and healthy development.

Sex education policy must reinforce the importance of healthy decisions. The goal is ultimately to make a positive change in cultural norms, similar to that reached by other successful public health campaigns. Teens need guidance from those who believe that they are capable of rising to the high expectations of risk avoidance and that even if they have made risky decisions in the past, they can make healthier ones in the future.

SRA education is a better approach, because it is built on sound theory and empirical evidence. Parents, teens, and others on both sides of the political aisle support it. Thus, SRA education must be the first line of defense in helping improve the health of teens.

Recommendations

- **Adopt sexual risk avoidance as a better approach to teenage pregnancy prevention**. Sexual risk avoidance should be the primary Federal strategy in preventing teenage pregnancy and STIs.
- **Support parents or other guardians in their responsibility to be the primary sex educators of their children.** Federal policy efforts should always support a positive relationship between parents and their children. Parents and guardians are critical to protecting children and teens from the consequences of risky behavior, especially sexual behavior.
- **Require a comprehensive evaluation plan for prevention programs.** To better understand the impact of an education model of prevention requires more than just an outcome evaluation. Program evaluation needs to be conducted over stages that begin with assessing needs, and then program development and design. Program design should be grounded in behavioral theory, logic, and research. Outcome evaluation should measure both short- and long-term outcomes of the program.
- **Increase public awareness that teens need guidance related to risky behavior, including sexual behavior.** Many parents, guardians, educators, and policy makers are not aware of adolescent developmental needs. Providing that information will make them more effective in providing appropriate guidance and protecting teens from the consequences of behaviors beyond their children's abilities.
- **Develop a national strategic plan to incorporate the SRA approach into all programs designed to prevent and treat teenage pregnancy.**

Appendix

SRA education has an impressive and growing body of research pointing to its effectiveness. To date, 22 peer-reviewed studies show statistically significant evidence of positive behavioral impact for students with all levels of sexual experience. Most research was obtained within the school setting. Results consistently reveal three noteworthy findings:

Compared to their peers, students in SRA programs are:

- Much more likely to delay sexual initiation.
- Much more likely to discontinue or decrease their sexual activity.
- No less likely to use a condom if they initiate sex.

A summary of each study is briefly described in the following table. More information on these studies can be found on the website of the National Abstinence Education Association.

Program	State	Main Results	Key: SRA program is in green[i]
Jemmott Study of Inner City Youth[ii]	Pennsylvania	Sex Initiation: • 32.6% that received abstinence intervention • 51.8% that received "safer sex" • 41.8% that received "comprehensive" sex education • 46.6% of the control	
Reasons of the Heart[iii]	Virginia	Program Group virgins 46% less likely than Comparison Group virgins to initiate sexual intercourse after one year.	

Game Plan/Aspire[iv]	California	• Significant gains for participants completing program in areas of "Intent to Practice Abstinence" and "Practice of Abstinence Behavior." • At 6-months, non-program participants 4x times as likely to engage in sexual activity.	
Choosing the Best[v]	Georgia	Program participant 43% less likely to initiate sex than non-program participant (21.6% vs. 11.5%).	
Heritage Keepers®: A Replication[vi]	Georgia	10.1% of Program Group initiated sex 10 months following program vs. 24.4% in the Comparison Group.	
Choosing the Best/ STARS Georgia[vii]	Georgia	• Control Group shows 9% increase pre-test to post-test of participants reporting ever having sex (28% to 37%). • Program Group establishes much lower increase pre-test to post-test of participants reporting every having sex (31% to 34%).	

L.I. Teen Freedom Program[viii]	New York	Program participants nearly 3 1/2 times (OR) more likely than average to maintain abstinence 12 months after participating in the program.	
The RIDGE Project, Inc.[ix]	Ohio	Of respondents expressing intention to abstain from all sexual activity until marriage, 93% overall and 34% of those previously sexually active, report no sexual activity on follow-up survey.	
Earle School District[x]	Arkansas	Since start of abstinence program in 2001, teen pregnancy in the senior class has dropped from 1 in 2 girls (2001) to 1 in 10 girls (2009).	

17

Arkansas Title V Funded Programs[xi]	Arkansas	Sexually experienced teens and sexually inexperienced male teens who received abstinence education were about twice as likely to be sexually abstinent one year later than those who did not.	
Sex Can Wait[xii]	Arkansas	At the high school level, statistically significant differences in treatment and comparison groups with students in the program group less likely to report participation in sexual activity ever or in the last month.	
Heritage Keepers[xiii]	South Carolina	Program virgins about one-half as likely as comparison group virgins to initiate sex by the 12-month follow-up.	

Best Friends[xiv]	Washington, DC	Program girls much more likely to abstain from sexual activity than YRBS respondents.	
Pure & Simple Lifestyle (PLS)[xv]	Kansas	• Increase in self-reported abstinence from pre to post-intervention. • Participants in the comparison group reported a decrease in the number of always-abstinent responses.	
Not Me Not Now[xvi]	New York	The adolescent pregnancy rate dropped from 63.4% to 49.5%.	

For Keeps[xvii]	Ohio	Sexually active students exposed to the intervention reported fewer episodes of sexual intercourse and fewer partners.	**Sexually Experienced Students: Program vs. Control** • Program students reported fewer multiple episodes of sexual intercourse • Program students reported fewer partners
Worth the Wait[xviii]	Texas	Teen pregnancy rate declined from 34.8% to 16.1%.	
Abstinence By Choice[xix]	Arkansas	• 5.9% of 8th grade girls in program group had initiated sexual activity compared to 10.2% in comparison group.	
Stay SMART[xx]	National	Reduced levels of recent sexual activity two years after program by youth who had engaged in prior sexual activity.	**Sexually Experienced Teens: Program vs. Control** – Program teens had more favorable attitudes toward sexual activity before the program but significantly less favorable attitudes after program. – Program teens had significantly less sexual BEHAVIOR at 27 month posttest.

Facts[xxi]	Oregon	Twelve-month transition rates from virgin to non-virgin status at one-year follow up significant.	
Teen Aid/Sex Respect[xxii]	Utah	High school students with low to medium levels of sexual values sexual initiation rate at 22% for program vs. 37% for control teens.	
Teen Aid Family Life Education Project[xxiii]	Washington	Reduced sexual initiation rates among high- risk high school students by more than one-fourth: 37% vs. 27% for control group.	

[i] Additional information, including charts are available from:

NAEA (2011). *Abstinence Works 2011*. Washington, D.C.: author.

[ii] Jemmott, J. B., Jemmott L. S.,Fong G. T. (2010). Efficacy of a theory-based abstinence-only intervention over 24 months. Arch Pediatr Adolesc Med. 2010;164(2):152-159.

[iii] Weed S., Ericksen I.H., Lewis A., Grant G.E., & Wibberly K.H. (2008). An abstinence program's impact on cognitive me- diators and sexual initiation. American Journal Health Behavior, 32(1):60-73.

[iv] Educational Evaluators, Inc. (2011) Evaluation Report of the Tesorosde Esperanza CBAE Evaluation report during 2008-09 project year. Program. -Impact Evaluation submitted to Department of Health and Human Services.

[v] Weed, S.E., & Ericksen I.H., (2008) What kind of abstinence education works? Comparing outcomes of two approaches. Submitted for publication.

[vi] Birch P. and Weed S. (2008). Effects of Heritage Keepers® Abstinence Education Program: A Replication. Salt Lake City: The Institute for Research & Evaluation.

[vii] Lieberman,LD,(December2010). Evaluation Report of the Choosing the Best, Inc./ STARS Georgia High School Abstinence Education Program, Submitted to HHS, ACYF under CBAE grant funding. Montclair, NJ: Montclair State University.

[viii] Rue,L.A, Chandran,R., Pannu,A., Bruce,D., Singh,R.(2010). Estimate of Program Effects, L.I. Teen Freedom Program. Program.-Impact Evaluation submitted to Department of Health and Human Services.

[ix] Seufert, R.L. & Campbell,D.G.(2010)The RIDGE Project Evaluation 2008-2010. Program.- Impact Evaluation submitted to Department of Health and Human Services.

[x] Rue, L. A., Rogers, J., Kinder, E., Bruce, D. (2009). Summative Evaluation: Abstinence Education Program. -Impact Evaluation submitted to Department of Health and Human Services, Grant # 90AE0219.

[xi] Birch P. and Weed S. (2008). Phase V Final Report: Delivered to the Arkansas Department of Health. July 16, 2008. Salt Lake City: The Institute for Research & Evaluation.

[xii] Denny, G., & Young, M. (2006). An evaluation of an abstinence-only sex education curriculum: An 18-month follow-up. Journal of School Health, 76 8): 414-422.

[xiii] Weed, S.E., Ericksen I.H., & Birch P.J. (2005). An evaluation of the Heritage Keepers Abstinence Education Program. Evaluating abstinence education programs: Improving implementation and assessing impact. Washington DC: DHHS, Office of Population Affairs and the Administration for Children and Families.

[xiv] Lerner, R., (2004). Can abstinence work? An analysis of the Best Friends Program. Adolescent and Family Health, 3(4), 185-192.

[xv] Wetta-Hall, R. (2010). Pure & Simple Lifestyle (PSL): Evaluation of Teen Participants of the Pure & Simple Choice Curriculum, Year Five Program Impact Evaluation submitted to HHS.

[xvi] Doniger, A., Adams, E., Utter, C. & Riley, J. (2001). Impact evaluation of the "Not Me, Not Now: Abstinence-oriented, adolescent pregnancy prevention communications pro- gram, Monroe County, New York. *Journal of Health Communications. 6,*45-60.

[xvii] Borawski, E.A.,Trapl E.S., Lovegreen, L.D., Colabianchi, N., & Block T. (2005). Effectiveness of abstinence-only intervention in middle school teens. *American Journal Health Behavior, 29*(5), 423-434.

[xviii] Tanner Jr.,J.F., & Ladd, R.N. (2005). Saturation Abstinence Education: An application of social marketing In Golden A (Ed.) Evaluating Abstinence Education Programs: Improving Implementation and Assessing Impact. Washington DC: Office of Population Affairs and the Administration for Children and Families. Dept of Health and Human Services.

[xix] Weed, S.E. (2001, October 15). Title V abstinence education programs: Phase I interim evaluation report to Arkansas Department of Health. Salt Lake City: Institute for Research and Evaluation.

[xx] St. Pierre, T.L., Mark, M.M., Kaltreider, D.L., & Aikin, K.J. (1995) A 27-month evaluation of sexual activity prevention program in Boys and Girls Clubs across the Nation. *Family Relations.* *44*(1): 69-77.

[xxi] Weed, S.E. (1994). FACTS Project: Year-end evaluation report, 1993-1994. Prepared for the Office of the Adolescent Pregnancy Prevention Programs, U.S. Department of Health and Human Services.

[xxii] Weed, S.E. (1992). Predicting and changing sexual activity rates: A comparison of three Title XX programs. Report submitted to OAPP, U.S. DHHS.

[xxiii] Weed, S.E., Prigmore, J., Tenas, R. (1992). The Teen Aid FLE Project: 5th year evaluation report. Report submitted to HHS.